Notes, Quotes & Advice

♦

San Diego's Most Famous and Successful People
Share Their Wit, Wisdom and Insights on Success

Written and Compiled by Lee T. Silber

Tales From The Tropics Publishing Co.
Del Mar, California

Copyright © 1994 by Lee T. Silber

All rights reserved. Written permission must be secured from the publisher to use or reproduce any part of this book, except for brief quotations in critical reviews or articles.

For information address Tales From The Tropics Publishing Co.
P.O. Box 4100-186, Del Mar, CA 92014.
(Books are available at special discounts for bulk purchases)
For more information, call 619/792-5312

Cover Design, Page Design and Layout by Lee T. Silber

ISBN: 0-9628771-2-3

Printed in San Diego, California, USA
First Edition

TABLE OF CONTENTS

◆

INTRODUCTION		vii
CHAPTER 1 ◆	Success	1
CHAPTER 2 ◆	Goals	8
CHAPTER 3 ◆	Adversity	16
CHAPTER 4 ◆	Optimism	23
CHAPTER 5 ◆	Courage	27
CHAPTER 6 ◆	Persistence	33
CHAPTER 7 ◆	Fitness	37
CHAPTER 8 ◆	Balance	42
CHAPTER 9 ◆	Career	47

CHAPTER 10 ◆ Effort	52
CHAPTER 11 ◆ Business	57
CHAPTER 12 ◆ San Diego	66
CHAPTER 13 ◆ Quotable	72

ALSO INCLUDED: The Twelve Most Common Characteristics of Highly Successful San Diegans   85

INTRODUCTION

WHAT if you could personally ask the most successful and famous people in San Diego how they achieved their success and what you could do to accomplish more and be more? And what if they offered you encouragement and insight based on their own experiences on their way to the top? How would you like to have Gregory Peck, Tony Gwynn, Ralph Rubio, Jonas Salk, Roger Hedgecock, Jenny Craig, Junior Seau and others as your personal mentors to help you in your search for success, fulfillment, wealth and health in your career and personal life? Well, now you can! In their own words San Diego's most famous and successful people share their secrets to success. This is an indispensable sourcebook of proven ways to aim high and achieve more.

This book is essential reading for successful people and would-be successful people everywhere. You will find these practical, inspirational quotations are invaluable for speakers, managers, teachers and entrepreneurs.

The statements in this book were chosen because they convey the most information in the fewest amount of words. Use them as personal motivators to comfort, clarify and give direction in your quest for success. Try to read at least one positive thought each and every day.

After each entry you will notice that credit is given to those who made the statement, their claim to fame or accomplishments as well as their connection to San Diego.

The final chapter of this book is devoted to exploring the twelve most common characteristics of highly successful people. These proven concepts are common factors that contributed to the success of many of those included in this book. These effective "what to do" and "how to do it" ideas can be used to learn and grow from, whether you seek success or simply want to maintain it.

Other books by Lee T. Silber

Successful San Diegans (1993)
The Guide to Dating in San Diego (1991)

SUCCESS

Chapter One

♦ NOTES, QUOTES & ADVICE ♦

It's a cinderella dream come true... It's amazing...It's not so much that my life has changed, it's that I am now able to experience things that were not accessible to me before... What I enjoy most are the simple things success provides. I can buy groceries, pay the rent and phone bills.

WHOOPI GOLDBERG
(Actress. Former San Diegan 1974-1982)

I know plenty of people who are successful financially, professionally, but they're not happy and they don't know what makes them happy because they're so carried away with trying to get to a certain point. The bottom line for me is I want to be happy.

HANK BAUER
(Sportscaster/Former Chargers Running Back)

◆ Notes, Quotes & Advice ◆

We so often are apt to judge our own success against other people's achievements. It really has to be an internal issue. You have to realize that given whatever limited resources and whatever the odds were that you did the best you possibly could. That's what success is.

LARRY HIMMEL
(Award-winning television personality. San Diegan since 1972)

I tell kids all the time that it's not the car, the clothes or the house that determines the quality of life you are going to have. It's what's inside that counts and very few people understand that, but the ones that do are wealthy people.

DAVID LLYOD
(Shipbuilder/Owner of Bay City Marine, Inc.)

◆ NOTES, QUOTES & ADVICE ◆

Certain professions simply come with higher salaries attached to them, and some people are in them and some people aren't. That doesn't mean you have to make a six-figure income to be a success.

STEVE KELLEY
(Union-Tribune editorial cartoonist)

The way I judge success is if you can walk away from whatever you do knowing that you have given everything you had, then you are a successful person.

TIM FLANNERY
(Former Padre infielder/minor league manager)

I feel successful each and every time I am able to finish what I started. It is that sense of accomplishment that I am continually striving for.

LEE SILBER
(Author/entrepreneur.)

◆ Notes, Quotes & Advice ◆

I'm not sure that I know what success means to me. I used to think that success meant not having to worry about money and being known to people. Fortune and fame. I suppose I have something like fame. My name is fairly well known in San Diego. I don't have fortune, but then I didn't choose a profession where many make a fortune. By those standards, one out of two isn't so bad.

TOM BLAIR
(Award-winning Union-Tribune columnist)

Success is peace of mind and a feeling of well-being within yourself.
NICK REYNOLDS
(Co-founder of the Kingston Trio. Coronado native)

I never gave success that much thought, but now that I'm older, I think about it more and I appreciate it more.

TED LEITNER
(Award-winning sportscaster/announcer)

◆ Notes, Quotes & Advice ◆

Success in and of itself was never my primary goal. The goal was to have a fullfilling life.

GABRIEL WISDOM
(Stockbroker/On-air personality)

My definition of success is to be happy, healthy and able to express myself fully and freely in doing work that I really enjoy and which benefits a great number of people. All material rewards are secondary.

BRIAN TRACY
(Author of *Maximum Achievement*/Solana Beach resident)

I am not one who measures success by wealth or what you own. Your family and children are far more important than how much money you accumulate.

GARY BISZANTZ
(Chairman of the board of Cobra Golf, Inc. of Carlsbad)

◆ Notes, Quotes & Advice ◆

Success - once you've achieved it, it's gone and you have to set the next goal. What they say in Hollywood is that you are only as good as your last film. In sports you're only as good as your last touchdown. In my business it's the same way.

CAROL LeBEAU
(Award-winning newscaster. San Diegan since 1981)

You never feel like you've gotten wherever it is you're trying to get to. Everytime you get to what you think is the top of the mountain, you realize it's just a plateau, so you're never going to see the top of that mountain. You're just going to reach plateaus over and over. It's really great to sit at each plateau and relax, but you can't do that very long because as soon as you do, everything starts to pass you by. Unless you keep moving up, that's all you are going to have.

ROBERT HAYS
(Television and film star. Honored by Grossmont College)

GOALS

Chapter Two

♦ NOTES, QUOTES & ADVICE ♦

If you don't set goals for yourself, you are doomed to achieve the goals of somebody else.

BRIAN TRACY
(Author/speaker/trainer/consultant)

Goals are always a priority for anyone to succeed because they help you focus on what you want.

JUNIOR SEAU
(Pro Bowl Charger Linebacker. Oceanside High graduate)

I don't think the formula for success ever really changes. You have to set optimistic goals, but never anything completely out of reach. Then you work your tail off.

STEVE KELLEY
(Editorial cartoonist/artist)

♦ NOTES, QUOTES & ADVICE ♦

Clear goals are imperative in order to go for and achieve anything. Goals allow you to put yourself in the right place at the right time.

IRA OPPER
(Award-winning producer/director/entrepreneur)

A small amount of ability, overwhelming desire, meaningful goals, and you can accomplish almost anything.

MIKE AMBROSE
(Weatherman/aka "Captain Mike")

Success starts with having a realistic goal. A lot of people make the mistake of having too lofty a goal. Start by putting one foot in front of the other.

GABRIEL WISDOM
(Former host of nationally syndicated radio program/stockbroker)

♦ Notes, Quotes & Advice ♦

I really believe in goals. I think the unhappiest points I've had in my life were when I didn't realize that I had achieved my goals and I had yet to set new ones. People who are unhappy and wondering how to get where they really want to go, need to set goals.

MIC MEAD
(CEO of Adventure 16. San Diegan since 1955)

The greatest time saver of all is the word 'No.' Use it for anything that does not advance you toward your goals.

BRIAN TRACY
(Author of *The Psychology of Success*)

You have to be flexible with your goals. I have never seen a goal go exactly the way I, or anybody else, planned it.

DAVID LLOYD
(Successful San Diego entrepreneur)

◆ NOTES, QUOTES & ADVICE ◆

I have never set unrealistic goals for myself. I think I have always been honest with what my talents and abilities are and I have set goals based on that, always taking little steps outside my comfort zone.

CAROL LeBEAU
(Award-winning newscaster)

To become successful you must first decide what it is you want out of life, then be disciplined and organized enough to set goals and constantly work towards those goals on an everyday basis.

LEE SILBER
(Author of *Successful San Diegans*)

You need to not only establish goals but also be able to structure them from a priority standpoint and constantly monitor your performance.

ANTHONY DeSIO
(Vice Chairman and CEO of Mailboxes Etc., Inc of San Diego)

◆ NOTES, QUOTES & ADVICE ◆

We were laughing recently while going through my high school album and where it says what do you want to be, I put a pro football player, so I did have a clear image of what I wanted to do. I spent all of my focus and concentration doing that.

ED WHITE
(Former Charger lineman/sculptor. San Diego native)

My goal was to be as good as I could be and to become one of the best.
SCOTT SIMPSON
(Pro golfer/winner of the 1987 U.S. Open. San Diego native)

It just started off as a flicker, an idea... then it became a goal. Then I set up a game plan and worked towards that goal. I made that dream come true, but not without a lot of hard work and dedication.

IVAN "IRONMAN" STEWART
(Off-road racing legend. Alpine resident)

♦ NOTES, QUOTES & ADVICE ♦

You have to remember that everything you do counts. If you read a book on success, that is points in your favor. If you watch TV in your spare time, that is wasting time because you are either moving towards your goals or away from them.

BRIAN TRACY
(Internationally known Author/speaker. Solana Beach resident)

The goal is the most important part of success. You can't be committed to a goal that you haven't yet set. Once you set that goal, then you commit yourself to it and you can go about accomplishing it.

DAVID LLOYD
(SBA Minority Small Business Person of the Year, 1990)

Don't ever stop and don't ever let anyone tell you can't achieve your goals.
LARRY HIMMEL
(From the Foreword to *Successful San Diegans*)

◆ Notes, Quotes & Advice ◆

Set a goal and work towards it. If I've said to myself once, I've said a million times - in the water and on land - stay with it, stay with it.

FLORENCE CHADWICK
(Record setting Channel swimmer. San Diego native)

I typed out my ultimate goal on a piece of paper, had it laminated and carry it with me in my wallet so that I can look at it whenever I have an idle moment. Because I look at it almost daily, I have found that it has become crystallized in my mind. It has also helped to clarify my thinking, making it easier to make decisions. When you know exactly what your ultimate goal is, you have a much clearer understanding of what you need to do each day to reach it.

LEE SILBER
(Publisher of the "Success in San Diego" newsletter)

ADVERSITY

Chapter Three

♦ Notes, Quotes & Advice ♦

Perseverance is about the only virtue outside of having fun at what you do that I think you can pinpoint as common to everyone who has been a success in any field.

ROGER HEDGECOCK
(Radio talk show host/Attorney)

If you really believe that you can make the best of any situation, then no matter how bad it is there is only one way out and that's up.

JEANNE JONES
(Internationally known cookbook author. La Jollan)

Things turn out best for those who make the best out of the way things turn out.

ART LINKLETTER
(TV and radio personality/speaker. San Diego native)

◆ NOTES, QUOTES & ADVICE ◆

I've never really had any tough times because I don't view them as tough times. I view them as new challenges and try to find solutions.
JUDI SHEPPARD MISSETT
(Founder of Jazzercise, Inc. of Carlsbad)

As people deal with major struggles, I'm convinced that most people would do anything just to get over them; whether it be a financial struggle, the break-up of a relationship, divorce or illness, whatever it is. But after major struggles like that, we come out of them changed people.
ROLF BENIRSCHKE
(Former Charger kicker. La Jolla High graduate)

Never give up. Never settle for for less than the best.
CORKY McMILLIN
(Home builder/Off-road racing champion.Sweetwater high graduate)

◆ Notes, Quotes & Advice ◆

The most important thing to learn in life with regard to what has happened to you is that it is not where you're coming from, but where you are going that matters most.

BRIAN TRACY
(Author/speaker/trainer/consultant)

Many people in hard times wallow in self pity, and I could never understand that.

DAVID LLOYD
(Self-made success story)

I am where I am for one reason. It's very simple. It's because I never stop going after it. I just don't stop despite the many frustrations along the way.

ART GOOD
(On -air personality/promoter/entrepreneur)

♦ NOTES, QUOTES & ADVICE ♦

If you're going to sit down and cry every time things go wrong, you're never going to get anywhere in life. It takes being able to get off your butt when you're down and not taking 'No' for an answer to make it.

JUNIOR SEAU
(All-Pro Charger linebacker)

When you are committed to something and things go wrong, the thought of bailing out never occurs.

DAVID LLOYD
(Ship builder)

You will undoubtedly get terribly discouraged no matter what you do. There's only one thing to do. Smile and keep moving, because when you move through those things you're going to find tremendous success.

ROGER HEDGECOCK
(Radio talk show host. St. Augustine High and SDSU graduate)

◆ NOTES, QUOTES & ADVICE ◆

As a football team our goal was to win the Super Bowl. Does that mean the other 27 teams that don't win the Super Bowl are failures? I don't think so. A lot of what we learned as individuals and as a team came about as we experienced very difficult times.

ROLF BENIRSCHKE
(KNSD spokesman/host of *Great Comebacks*)

As much as you hate going through the tough times, and I've been through the toughest times you can imagine, the fact is the wisdom and poise and perspective I gained from it was priceless. You just have to smile and remain upbeat, keep your hand on the tiller and head through the stormy times with an eye towards the other end and better times ahead. And when you get there - and you will get there - you will appreciate those better days more than you ever did before.

ROGER HEDGECOCK
(Radio talk show host/author)

◆ Notes, Quotes & Advice ◆

There have been times when I haven't gotten anything that I've wanted or anything that resembles what I wanted, but I have always been able to pick myself up by the bootstraps and go forward.

TAWNY KITAEN
(Host of *America's Funniest People*. San Diego native)

I was collecting $47 a week unemployment, then I lost the unemployment because I got a job making $45 a week. I was living in my van. I look back on that stuff and I wouldn't give it up for anything.

ROBERT HAYS
(Actor. Former San Diegan)

I have learned that although life doesn't always seem fair, it is always worth fighting for.

ROLF BENIRSCHKE
(Speaker/former Charger kicker)

OPTIMISM

Chapter Four

◆ NOTES, QUOTES & ADVICE ◆

There are always going to be stumbling blocks along the way. Just look at it as a challenge and rather than a negative, turn it into a positive and say, 'What good can come of it?'

JULIE MANNIS
(Publisher of *Beach and Bay Press* and the *Peninsula Beacon*)

I'm very persistent. I will not be squelched!

GLORIA PENNER
(Director of KPBS-TV)

I looked down and saw blood all over my jersey and I said, 'Hey! Did I hurt Somebody?'

MARCUS ALLEN
(What he said after having his nose broken in practice at USC.)

◆ NOTES, QUOTES & ADVICE ◆

I think life is a combination of highs and lows, and I try to just focus on the high points.

ED WHITE
(Former Charger lineman. Julian resident)

As golfers say, 'When you're playing good, you don't think of hitting a bad shot and when you're playing poorly you never think you'll hit a good shot.' My advice is to always think 'Good shot.'

GARY BISZANTZ
(Chairman of the board of Cobra Golf, Inc.)

I didn't worry about the things I had no control over, like playing every day. I could have sat on the bench and been miserable. Instead I gave everything I had whenever I got a chance to play.

TIM FLANNERY
(Former utility infielder)

◆ Notes, Quotes & Advice ◆

Lee Travino is an incurable optimist. Don't try to tell him he is anything but the best, he just doesn't know any better. I see it as real confidence, brought about by the habit of enthusiasm, which is optimism in action.

DENIS WAITLEY
(Best-selling author. San Diego native)

There are really only three ways to look at a situation. You can either be negative, indifferent or you can be positive and optimistic. Successful people almost always choose to be positive, hopeful and optimistic.

LEE SILBER
(Author/entrepreneur. San Diegan since 1975)

I have a great time wherever I am, whatever I am doing.

ROBERT HAYS
(Starred in hit movie *Airplane!*)

COURAGE

Chapter Five

◆ NOTES, QUOTES & ADVICE ◆

I think anything is possible. The fear many times is just thinking about something and creating a picture of a mountain that is so huge to overcome, whatever it might be. Try taking a little bit at a time, set a direction and do what you say you're going to do.

MARTIN KRUMING
(Editor of the San Diego Daily Transcript)

You overcome the fear (of speaking in public) by just doing it, actually doing it. I started in college speaking at banquets. Now I love the reaction from a live audience.

TED LEITNER
(Sportscaster/announcer/media celebrity)

No matter what happens on the diving board, my mom's gonna love me.
GREG LOUGANIS
(Olympic Gold Medalist/diving champion. San Diego native)

◆ NOTES, QUOTES & ADVICE ◆

The only way to overcome fear is to do the thing you fear and by doing it a lot. Keep pitting yourself against it all the time and you get used to dealing with fear. That's the only way to overcome it.

BRAD GERLACH
(Professional surfer. North county resident)

For me it was always the fear of failure. If I did not get up and make that speech in my speech class, then I really would be a failure. At least if I got up there and made the effort, there was a chance that I would succeed.

CAROL LeBEAU
(Award-winning newscaster)

Even if you're petrified, don't let it show. Don't let them know you're afraid.
RUSS T. NAILZ
(Comedian. Advice he received from Larry Himmel)

◆ NOTES, QUOTES & ADVICE ◆

Many people talk about what it is they want to do. Some even intend to do it. But it is the the select few who overcome their fears and take appropriate action that are the ones who achieve success and reach their goals.

LEE SILBER
(Author/entrepreneur)

They (San Diego's early movers and shakers) saw opportunities, they saw possibilities, and they didn't dwell on why it couldn't be done.

KEN KRAMER
(Radio talk show host/producer)

Fighting is a lot easier than public speaking. I was really honored that they asked me to speak, but I've never had butterflies like this.

TERRY NORRIS
(WBC Boxer of the Year. Alpine resident)

◆ Notes, Quotes & Advice ◆

I was determined I was going to become more friendly no matter how painful it was, and I started by forcing myself to say hello to people. I had a goal and I saw what it would take to achieve that goal - that I couldn't be shy any longer, and I had to force myself to overcome the fear. It changed my life.

MARY-ELLEN DRUMMOND
(Author/speaker. Long-time San Diegan)

If you see something you want, overcome your fears and move forward and do the necessary things to make it happen.

"SHOTGUN TOM" KELLY
(On-Air personality. Mt. Miguel High graduate)

No Fear/No Limits.

NO FEAR
(T-Shirt/No Fear is a Carlsbad-based company)

◆ NOTES, QUOTES & ADVICE ◆

You don't hear too many self doubts from successful people. They know what they're doing, they're organized, and they knew what they wanted and they went after it.

GLORIA PENNER
(KPBS-TV producer/director. San Diegan since 1969)

The fear you learn in surfing and the challenge of pushing the limits and pulling it off create a feeling of exhilaration. The thrill and rush of adrenaline created by going a little further than your mind thinks you should and the knowledge from that experience give you the edge in the real world and can help get you through situations that would be impossible for someone who hasn't pushed the fear factor.

IRA OPPER
(Owner of Frontline Video & Film of Del Mar)

PERSISTENCE

Chapter Six

◆ Notes, Quotes & Advice ◆

Never say die. Be stubborn. Be persistent. Anything worth having is worth striving for with all your might.

ORVILLE REDENBACHER
(Popcorn magnate. Coronado resident since 1977)

I would never quit. I was always the last one to take the (boxing) gloves off and that was only because I wanted to, not because I wanted to quit.

JESSE VALDEZ
(Olympic boxer/award-winning cameraman/entrepreneur)

If anybody said to me 'You can't do it,' I'd tell them they just didn't know Mic Mead.

MIC MEAD
(Owner of San Diego-based Adventure 16)

◆ NOTES, QUOTES & ADVICE ◆

Determination is the wake-up call to the human will.
ANTHONY ROBBINS
(Author/entrepreneur/trainer. Del Mar resident)

There were always coaches who said that I couldn't do something. I couldn't throw, I couldn't hit with power, I couldn't run, I couldn't field my position, or whatever. I think that's one of the reasons I've been successful, because they can measure everything you do on the field but they can't measure what's inside of you and what drives you.
TONY GWYNN
(Baseball star. Poway resident)

Both Bob and Bret were mentally tough kids who had the desire to play baseball and weren't affected by temporary setbacks.
RAY BOONE
(Only family to have three generations play Major League baseball)

♦ Notes, Quotes & Advice ♦

People said I couldn't make it in the NFL. I was too small, too slow, came from a small school. But I did! Not only did I make it, but I lasted and I excelled. People would say, 'Look at this guy, he's an overachiever. How can this guy do the things he's doing?' There's no secret. I did it with determination and hard work.

HANK BAUER
(Sportscaster/former Charger. San Diegan since 1977)

In those days, it (polio) was nearly a death sentence, or at the very least confinement to a wheelchair. They told my dad he would never walk again, and he told them that he had to - he had a family and he had work to do. He got up and was able to walk out of sheer determination. He's an amazing role model for me.

ROGER HEDGECOCK
(Radio talk show host/attorney/author)

FITNESS

Chapter Seven

◆ Notes, Quotes & Advice ◆

I resent it when people think I've never had to work at looking good, as if I were anointed with a magic wand. What people see is the result of a lot of discipline and effort on my part.

RAQUEL WELCH
(Actress/performer/fitness fanatic. La Jolla native)

Eating properly costs less money, and you can exercise by getting out and going for a real good walk every morning. You don't have to join a fancy gym. You don't have to buy expensive food. It's the only thing in today's economy where less money can actually buy you a better life.

JEANNE JONES
(Internationally respected diet consultant)

A waist is a terrible thing to mind.

TERRY FORSTER
(Former major league pitcher. Santana High grad.).

◆ Notes, Quotes & Advice ◆

My belief to this day is if you want to change your life, the first place to start is in the physical area.

ANTHONY ROBBINS
(Author/entrepreneur)

How do you feel today? If you don't feel terrific there is something wrong, and it's probably that you aren't eating right or you aren't getting enough exercise.

JEANNE JONES
(Author/columnist)

A person who is healthy and feels good has it all and should feel blessed every day. You can own a lot of things and be very wealthy, but lose your health and then absolutely nothing means anything.

GARY BISZANTZ
(Cobra Golf, Inc.).

◆ Notes, Quotes & Advice ◆

There are so many things a lot of us take for granted, for instance being healthy and happy and living in San Diego.

GABRIEL WISDOM
(Stock broker)

Once you start getting adequate amounts of exercise and start eating a reasonable, healthy diet, you're going to feel so much better that it becomes addictive. And yes, you will fall off, because as human beings we have choice, and because we have choice we often times make the wrong choices. But if you stay out too late too much, drink too much and don't exercise, you don't feel good, and when you know what it's like to feel terrific, you're not going to permanently give it up.

JEANNE JONES
(Author/columnist)

◆ Notes, Quotes & Advice ◆

Things always need adjustment and change. That's part of life. When you're younger, a little extra weight might look voluptuous. When you're older, it just looks like extra pounds.

RAQUEL WELCH
(Actress/former "Fairest of the Fair" winner in 1958)

I won't let a cold invade my body. I reject it. Some people will just lay down and say, okay, cold, come and get me and kick my butt. I say just the opposite. Get the hell out of my body, there's no place for you here.

DAVID LLOYD
(Hasn't missed more than 10 days of work in over 25 years)

BALANCE

Chapter Eight

◆ Notes, Quotes & Advice ◆

Because I have been somewhat obsessive and driven in the past to accomplish things, success really would be, in the end, being able to back off a little bit and start enjoying the fruits of my labor instead of continually trying to stack up more and more points.

SCOTT TINLEY
(Triathlete/entrepreneur. Del Mar resident)

Life is a journey and not a destination. If we make it a destination we never get there. The joy of the journey is what it's all about.

ROLF BENIRSCHKE
(1983 NFL Man of the Year)

It's (success) not all about money and career advancement, but a healthy balance between work and family.

GAIL STOORZA GILL
(Businesswoman/community leader)

♦ Notes, Quotes & Advice ♦

The challenge is to stay as balanced as possible between being married, having children, running a business, staying healthy, and keeping friends.

LISA T. RICHARDS
(Founder of San Diego-based Picnic People, Inc.)

I think everyone needs to find a passion that is outside of their normal reality and is total fun. That is one of the ways to keep your life balanced.

ANTHONY ROBBINS
(Author of *Unlimited Power*)

The key to a happy and productive life is being able to achieve a healthy balance between work and play and living for today and planning for tomorrow.

LEE SILBER
(Author/entrepreneur)

◆ Notes, Quotes & Advice ◆

Surfing is something I did all along, even when I played baseball. It balanced out the major league life and crazy lifestyle, the pressures and the stress. I knew when baseball was over surfing was always going to be there.

TIM FLANNERY
(Former Padre. Leucadia resident)

I got sucked into that whole superwoman thing in the 1980s where you think you have to have it all. Thank goodness we're in the nineties, because the eighties were a travesty. Women were exhausted. They were lonely. They had anxiety disorders, relationships that were in shambles and kids who were on drugs.

CAROL LeBEAU
(Newscaster)

◆ NOTES, QUOTES & ADVICE ◆

When I was on my deathbed, I came to the realization that careers and success and all the things that we worked so hard for all our lives and spend all our time and energy on are really not important.

STEVE LAURY
(Recording artist who is a cancer survivor)

I often imagine myself to be a very old lady, and think, what will matter? Very few things will matter. I don't want to live like 'Nothing matters, we're all going to die anyway,' and yet at the same time that's true. The trick is knowing what's important and what's not, what matters and doesn't matter, what to sweat and what to let go.

ANNETTE BENING
(Award-winning actress. Patrick Henry High graduate)

CAREER

Chapter Nine

◆ NOTES, QUOTES & ADVICE ◆

I never, never wanted to quit. I reached some low points where I thought 'Oh, God, it will never happen' and I got panicky. But I knew this (acting) was what I wanted to do and I wouldn't be happy doing anything else.

DAVID LEISURE
(Actor/aka "Joe Isuzu." Grossmont High grad.)

I see it over and over again in people who are successful. Number one and the absolute foremost thing is that they are having fun at what they do.

ROGER HEDGECOCK
(Radio talk show host/TV commentator)

I was a complete flop at getting a regular job.

FRANK CAPRA
(Legendary filmmaker/*It's a Wonderful Life*. Resided in Fallbrook)

◆ Notes, Quotes & Advice ◆

I couldn't be happier. I am doing exactly what I want to do - When you go out and work hard for something and you make it happen, you really appreciate it.

IVAN "IRONMAN" STEWART
(Off-road racing pioneer)

It was just another job to be done in a field in which I was interested.

JONAS SALK
(Medical pioneer who developed polio vaccine in 1955)

A lot of people feel so terrible about themselves that they never pursue the talents they have. And every human being has talent. The trick is finding it and knowing it once you've found it.

CLEAVON LITTLE
(Actor/*Blazing Saddles*. Kearny High graduate)

◆ Notes, Quotes & Advice ◆

Passion is the genesis of genius.

ANTHONY ROBBINS
(Author of *Awaken The Giant Within*)

Being successful means being happy with what you do everyday.

JUDI SHEPPARD MISSETT
(Jazzercise founder)

I enjoy being able to have control over what I do - controlling the product, controlling creativity and being in control of my own affairs rather than being beholden to others for employment. Success is being able to do what I want to do and being able to live the lifestyle I idealize for myself.

DAVE DREXLER
(Announcer/entrepreneur. Crawford High graduate)

◆ NOTES, QUOTES & ADVICE ◆

Do you know any person who has achieved massive success by doing what he hates? I don't. One of the keys to success is making a successful marriage between what you do and what you love.

ANTHONY ROBBINS
(Best selling author)

I find that I could work twenty-four hour days if I let myself. It's exciting, it's challenging and I love it - and when you love something, it's hard to stop.

MARY-ELLEN DRUMMOND
(Author/speaker/entrepreneur)

If success is judged by monetary gain, then I wouldn't qualify, but that's not the motivation to do what I do.

GEORGE VARGA
(Union-Tribune music critic)

EFFORT

Chapter Ten

◆ Notes, Quotes & Advice ◆

How much do you want it (success), because you'll have to work hard at what you want. It's that simple. If you're not willing to do that, then you're probably not going to get it.

WHOOPI GOLDBERG
(Once worked at the Big Kitchen Restaurant in Golden Hill)

Try to do every job a little better than everybody else.

DAVID LLOYD
(Shipbuilder)

There is no shortcut to success. Nothing but hard work, period. The guys I've been around that have excelled and that have lasted in any arena are those guys that have put in that extra work.

HANK BAUER
(Sportscaster)

◆ Notes, Quotes & Advice ◆

I think luck is to a certain degree a function of determination. I think if you work hard enough at something, you will end up getting a few breaks along the way.

STEVE KELLEY
(Union-Tribune editorial cartoonist)

It doesn't matter how much I'm getting paid for a job. I take it with the same degree of seriousness and put the same amount of effort into it.

DAVE DREXLER
(Owner of Voices Unlimited, a radio-commercial company)

It's easy to cheat yourself and just do enough to get by, but that's what everybody can do, just enough to get by. But those who want to be successful and maintain that level of success have got to push a little bit harder and do a little bit more.

TONY GWYNN
(Gold Glove outfielder)

◆ Notes, Quotes & Advice ◆

The thing that frustrates me most about young people is they want to get ahead but they aren't willing to work hard for it. They just do enough to get by, but they lack initiative. That's one of the major reasons I got ahead - I always took the initiative.

GAIL STOORZA GILL
(CEO and chairman of Stoorza, Ziegaus & Metzger, Inc.)

My basic premise for playing baseball is, if you work hard, good things will happen, and for the last eleven years I've worked very hard and things have happened for me that I didn't believe could happen.

TONY GWYNN
(Four-time batting champion)

The secret to success is goal setting, persistence, hard work, enthusiasm and doing what you like to do best.

ART LINKLETTER
(Best selling author/*Kids Say the Darndest Things*)

◆ Notes, Quotes & Advice ◆

My father instilled in me the fact that if somebody is going to take a chance on you and offer you a position, you owe it to them to give them your all.

MICHAEL McGEATH
(Founder of Fio's, downtown's award-winning restaurant)

Dreams don't become reality without a lot of hard work.

PETE WILSON
(Governor of the state of California/Former Mayor of San Diego)

I love what I do. It's that simple. And when you thoroughly enjoy your work, you never get tired of it.

SUZY SPAFFORD
(Creator of San Diego-based Suzy's Zoo greeting card company)

Business

Chapter Eleven

◆ Notes, Quotes & Advice ◆

When we started in business we never thought about failing, I mean really, the worst thing that could happen is we would have to go back to work, and at least that way we'd get two days off a week!

DAN HAMEL
(Founder of Hamel's Action Sports Center)

If there is any one key to success in business, I think it's delegation. Hire the best people you can, pay them accordingly and then trust them.

MIC MEAD
(CEO of San Diego-based Adventure 16 stores)

A lot of people have ideas and a lot of people have money, but to succeed in business you have to have a 'go for it' attitude.

RALPH RUBIO
(Rubio's Restaurants, Inc.)

◆ NOTES, QUOTES & ADVICE ◆

To be a successful entrepreneur, you have to be a competitive person who likes challenges, likes work, and can face disappointments.

GARY BISZANTZ
(Cobra Golf, Inc./champion race horse breeder)

You don't necessarily need a growing market to do well, you just need to do extremely well within your own market.

MIC MEAD
(Entrepreneur)

If you aren't willing to really roll up your sleeves and work hard, you probably should continue to work for somebody else. You must put a lot of time and effort into your business in order for it to be successful.

ANTHONY DeSIO
(President and CEO of Mailboxes Etc., Inc. San Diegan since 1978)

◆ Notes, Quotes & Advice ◆

The best way to succeed in business is to have people around you who are excellent. I have always tried to hire people who were smarter than myself, people who would work harder and were at least as dedicated as I was.

JACK GOODALL
(President, CEO and chairman of Foodmaker, Inc.)

Business is far more than making money. It can be developed into an art.
GEORGE MARSTON
(San Diego businessman/civic leader (1850-1946))

I think determination is the biggest attribute of a successful entrepreneur.

ANTHONY DeSIO
(*Inc. Magazine's* San Diego Entrepreneur of the Year 1989)

♦ Notes, Quotes & Advice ♦

Our growth has been a lot like a bulldozer moving forward, not too fast, but nothing can stop us.

JOSE da ROSA
(President and CEO of San Diego-based Balboa Travel, Inc.)

It's really hard when you first go out on your own to convince somebody to believe in you. You just have to keep believing in yourself even though people keep rejecting you.

MICHAEL McGEATH
(Founder of Fio's Cucina Italiana)

You have to realize that every business has periods of up times and periods of down times. It's just a normal cycle. You have the real good peaks and then you have the valleys.

JUDI SHEPPARD MISSETT
(In 1986 was named Top Woman Entrepreneur by the SBA)

♦ Notes, Quotes & Advice ♦

Being successful means creating products with significantly greater satisfaction to customers. Everyone wants a better product. Companies should give it to 'em!

ELY CALLAWAY
(Chairman and CEO of Carlsbad-based Callaway Golf Co.)

Success is where preparation and opportunity cross.

JENNY CRAIG
(President of Jenny Craig Weight Loss Centers)

Easy money. This may happen occasionally in business, but it's the exception rather than the rule. If anyone tells you that starting a business is easy, either they've never started one, they were lucky, or they're running a psychological con game.

JACK DUNNING
(Author/publisher/entrepreneur)

◆ Notes, Quotes & Advice ◆

A great store is more than a shop, it's a kind of institution, serving the community not only in business, but in civic affairs.

GEORGE MARSTON
(Founder of Marston's Department Store, August 8, 1878)

One thing people say to me all the time about starting a business is, 'I've got a good idea, but I'm not going to quit my job to go into it because I'm worried something might go wrong.' Well, I'm going to tell you right now, you don't have to worry about that, don't think about it, because it's going to happen.

DAVID LLOYD
(1983 SBA Contractor of the Year)

◆ Notes, Quotes & Advice ◆

I can't imagine myself ever going to work for somebody else, because I've always been in charge of my own destiny.

MICHAEL BRAU
(Founder of the Baltimore Bagel Co.)

I did a little bit every day towards my goal of starting my own business. I didn't do anything big, but I accomplished an item or two every day. I worked with my computer here. I went to school there. I bought a book. I had made it happen-not in one giant step, but in thousands of tiny steps.

JACK DUNNING
(Publisher of *ComputerEdge* magazine)

If you can laugh with a client, you'll probably do business with that client.

MARY-ELLEN DRUMMOND
(Polished Presentations)

◆ Notes, Quotes & Advice ◆

I do not think there are any other qualities so essential to the success of a business in the '90s as creativity, vision and imagination. The combination of those skills gives the entrepreneur the ability to compete in today's highly competitive and ever changing marketplace.

LEE SILBER
(Author/entrepreneur)

Unless you have the leadership capability to get your people to understand why achievement of your goals is important and get them all dedicated to that achievement, you'll never make it.

ANTHONY DeSIO
(Inducted into the Entrepreneur Hall of Fame)

If you get a chance to work for yourself, don't work for somebody else!

RAY RUBIO
(1993 winner of the SBA's Entrepreneurial Success Award)

SAN DIEGO

Chapter Twelve

◆ Notes, Quotes & Advice ◆

If I begin to reminisce about La Jolla, it sounds like another century. There were 2,000 people when I was a kid. People didn't even have street addresses; they had names on their houses.

GREGORY PECK
(Actor/born in La Jolla on April 5, 1916)

Science is the art of our times...San Diego can become the center of today's art just as surely as Florence was the center of the art of the Renaissance.

ROGER REVELLE
(San Diego statesman of science)

After traveling in all fifty states, this is the best place to live all year round.

ORVILLE REDENBACHER
(Coronado's "Popcorn King")

◆ Notes, Quotes & Advice ◆

I sent samples of my work to two metropolitan papers that were looking for cartoonists, The Omaha World Herald and The San Diego Union. When both offered me jobs, I chose to come to San Diego. Not a tough choice there. I flipped a coin and it came up Omaha. So I flipped it again.

STEVE KELLEY
(Union-Tribune editorial cartoonist)

I see people fighting to continue to keep San Diego a very special and unique place. I think that's what we have to continue to do.

JUDI SHEPPARD MISSETT
(Founder of Jazzercise. North county resident)

Because of my business, I could live anywhere in the world. I want to live and I choose to live here.

ANTHONY ROBBINS
(The best selling author lives in a 1924 castle overlooking Del Mar)

◆ Notes, Quotes & Advice ◆

If you talk doom and gloom all the time, before you know it you're keyed into that kind of thinking. I'm not ready to give up on San Diego yet. I would rather focus on the positives.

DAN HAMEL
(Hamel's Action Sports Center founded in 1967)

I've been here since 1955, and while I was in the building game we experienced a turnaround much like what's happening today. We got caught with projects that we couldn't sell for their financing, but San Diego came back, and it's going to come back again.

MIC MEAD
(Adventure 16 CEO. Long-time San Diegan)

Long-term, San Diego has to prosper simply because of its geography.
JACK GOODALL
(Foodmaker CEO. San Diego native)

◆ Notes, Quotes & Advice ◆

I think when people talk about the problems with our city they are comparing San Diego to what it used to be, wishing San Diego could continue as a place time forgot or as an elegant cul de sac, and they're really dreaming. We long ago passed the point of no return. San Diego is not a little town anymore.

JOSE da ROSA
(Balboa Travel CEO. San Diego native)

I get so discouraged when people are so negative about this city. Yes, we have problems, but I think we still have a very bright future.

LISA T. RICHARDS
(Founder of Picnic People, Inc./Community leader)

San Diego is a great place to live. This is where I want to be.

TONY GWYNN
(All Star outfielder. Poway resident)

◆ Notes, Quotes & Advice ◆

I think La Jolla is one of the prettiest places in the country. When I realized I could live any place in the world I wanted, and by choice I wanted to stay in San Diego, that is when I decided I'm a San Diegan.

JEANNE JONES
(Author. La Jollan)

When I was growing up here, it was wonderful. Imagine San Diego with half the population. It was a time when things seemed a lot simpler, a lot more one-dimensional. Sure, there were hardly any good restaurants back then, but who could afford good restaurants anyway? We lived simply and we enjoyed the simple pleasures of the San Diego lifestyle.

ROGER HEDGECOCK
(St. Augustine High graduate)

QUOTABLE

Chapter Thirteen

◆ Notes, Quotes & Advice ◆

Scientists believe that the universe is made of hydrogen because they claim it's the most plentiful ingredient. I claim that the most plentiful ingredient is stupidity.

FRANK ZAPPA
(Musician. Attended Grossmont High and Mission Bay High)

Baseball is the only field of endeavor where a man can succeed three times out of ten and be considered a good performer.

TED WILLIAMS
(Hall of Fame slugger. San Diego native)

It isn't that gentlemen really prefer blondes, it's just that we look dumber.

ANITA LOOS
(Author of *Gentlemen Prefer Blondes*. Attended San Diego High)

♦ Notes, Quotes & Advice ♦

When you're green, you're growing. When you're ripe, you rot.

RAY KROC
(Founder, McDonald's Corp./former Padres owner)

Money is an energy and if you don't use it wisely, you will eventually lose it.

GABRIEL WISDOM
(Stock broker)

There are plenty of successful people with minimal talent, and there are plenty of incredibly talented people with limited success.

GEORGE VARGA
(Union-Tribune music critic)

◆ NOTES, QUOTES & ADVICE ◆

When I was a little boy, I wanted to be a baseball player and join the circus. With the Yankees I accomplished both.

GRAIG NETTLES
(Yankee third baseman 1973-83. San Diego native)

Kids tell me they have problems. When I ask what their problem is - they say they don't have the money to do this or that. I tell them to learn to do the best job they can and the rest will take care of itself.

DENNIS HOPPER
(Actor/Director . Helix High graduate)

If you have to tell them who you are, you aren't anybody.

GREGORY PECK
(On fame. Co-founder of the La Jolla Playhouse in 1947)

◆ Notes, Quotes & Advice ◆

We've got to have a dream if we are going to make a dream come true.
DENIS WAITLEY
(Best selling author/speaker)

The people we admire in our lives are ordinary people that have been able to accomplish some extraordinary things. The things that make them extraordinary are things that we all possess.
ROLF BENIRSCHKE
(Former host of *Wheel of Fortune*)

You never ask why you've been fired because if you do, they're liable to tell you.
JERRY COLEMAN
(Broadcaster /1949 American League Rookie of the Year . La Jollan)

◆ NOTES, QUOTES & ADVICE ◆

It (money) means a certain freedom and a certain security. I think all of us have the fear of someday ending up a bag lady.

TAWNY KITAEN
(Co-starred in the movie *Bachalor Party*. San Diego native)

I can't sing or dance and I was never much of an actor... if I had talent I'd probably be unbearable.

ART LINKLETTER
(Celebrity. SDSU graduate)

By bringing positive things into other peoples' lives, I think your own life becomes enriched. When I can reach out to other people, whether in business or a personal situation, and see them grow, I take my greatest pleasure.

DIANA LINDSAY
(Author/publisher/entrepreneur)

◆ Notes, Quotes & Advice ◆

Art is about making something out of nothing and selling it.
FRANK ZAPPA
(Musician/composer/producer. Former San Diegan)

I suppose that persistence and stubbornness were responsible for my success. For years I was told I was looking for a will-o'-the-wisp, to leave well enough alone. I didn't listen. When someone tells me something can't be done, that's exactly what I'm going to do!
ORVILLE REDENBACHER
(Popcorn magnate)

We live by the Golden Rule. Those who have the gold make all the rules.
BUZZIE BAVASI
(Dodgers general manager, 1951-1968. La Jollan)

◆ Notes, Quotes & Advice ◆

As a shy, skinny kid, I wasn't outgoing at all. I didn't want to say anything because I didn't want to be rejected. I wasn't sure of myself when I was younger, but once I got a grasp of who I am, I started to open up. Now I run my mouth with the best of them!

TONY GWYNN
(Nine-time National League All Star)

I want to make it harder for the rich to grow richer and easier for the poor to keep from growing poorer.

E.W. SCRIPPS
(Owner of over 45 newspapers. (1854-1926)

One out of five Americans is unable to read this sentence.
AD FOR GENERAL DYNAMICS

◆ Notes, Quotes & Advice ◆

I'm So Miserable Without You It's Almost Like Having You Here
STEPHEN BISHOP
(Singer/songwriter. San Diego native)

Who would believe that an adopted kid of Samoan heritage, who was laughed at in school because he talked funny, would one day be spoken of in the same breath as Jesse Owens.

GREG LOUGANIS
(After being honored by the Jesse Owens Foundation)

Frankly, my early life doesn't fit very well with people's idea of Gregory Peck. There were hard times. Often I was flat broke, and sometimes I would sleep in Central Park. The only rich thing about me was my first name - Eldred. My mother found it in the phone book.

GREGORY PECK
(Born in La Jolla on April 5, 1916)

♦ NOTES, QUOTES & ADVICE ♦

The ability to delay gratification is always the biggest single challenge on the road to success.

BRIAN TRACY
(Author/speaker/trainer/consultant)

I don't think it's a great idea for these people to be telling everybody that they had a drug problem, but they don't have it anymore because they've gone three months sober. The idea of being in an anonymous twelve-step program is to stay anonymous. It's not good for other people if you slip.

DENNIS HOPPER
(Actor/director. Began his acting career at the Old Globe)

I'm patient. I'm patient in traffic. Jigsaw puzzles are my favorite hobby. Hell, my three children don't even bother me.

RANDY MILLIGAN
(Reds first baseman and a San Diego native)

◆ Notes, Quotes & Advice ◆

The best thing you can invest in is a good reputation.

CORKY McMILLIN
(1991 Builder of the Year, *California Builder* magazine)

I will never forget what my father said about my ambitions to go into radio. He said that I would never make it to first base. I knew that not only was I going to make it to first base, I was going to succeed in ways he never dreamed of.

MIKE AMBROSE
(Weatherman)

My grandmother was a lady. My mother is one of the girls. I'm a woman. My daughter is a doctor.

NATASHA JOSEFOWITZ
(Author/speaker/syndicated columnist. La Jollan)

◆ NOTES, QUOTES & ADVICE ◆

Co-workers say I hardly work at all, yet I'm always hearing from listeners and viewers that I work too hard. I work frequently. I don't work hard - I work often.

TED LEITNER
(In 1987 was voted the country's best sportscaster)

I see a lot of people who want to be successful, but they never take action on the things they learn. They'll say, 'I could do that!' but they don't do it. It's the ten percent I see who take action and take risks who are successful.

MARY-ELLEN DRUMMOND
(Author of *Fearless and Flawless Public Speaking*)

I have always found inspiration, insight, and hope from reading the success stories of others. It can make the impossible seem possible.

LEE SILBER
(President of Tales From The Tropics Publishing Co.)

◆ Notes, Quotes & Advice ◆

I believe that dreams are likely to lead to the betterment of the world. The imaginative child will become the imaginative man or woman most apt to invent, and therefore to foster, civilization.

L. FRANK BAUM
(Author of *The Wonderful Wizard of Oz*. Wintered in Coronado)

I'm not OK, you're not OK and that's OK!

NATASHA JOSEFOWITZ
(Nationally syndicated columnist/author)

Adults are obsolete children.

DR. SEUSS
(Aka Theodor Geisel. La Jollan)

The Twelve Most Common Characteristics Of Highly Successful San Diegans

Chapter Fourteen

1. Clearly Defined Goals

Successful people understand that in order to realize their dreams they have to set and achieve worthwhile goals. To them, setting clear, believable, written goals was the difference between success and failure. With meaningful goals, they were able to accomplish more and were more satisfied with their lives. Their goals gave them purpose and a focus for their talent and energy so they could structure their time towards reaching their objectives. They chose goals that inspired and excited them and were able to enjoy the process of working towards them. For most, the first step on the way to success was to clearly define their primary goals. They took the time to carefully select goals that were challenging and enabled them to make use of their talents and skills.

GOALS: *Cont'd...*

Once they were aware of the outcome they desired, these men and women were able to formulate a plan for getting there. Having a plan with a timetable for its accomplishment enabled them to focus on doing the most important thing toward their goals at any given time. Their plans included setting a series of short and medium-range goals. Step-by-step, they moved closer to achieving their long range goals. The plan added aim and energy to their lives, but it also required action and plenty of hard work and discipline to make their dreams a reality. They were willing to pay the price and make the short-term sacrifices necessary for long-term prosperity. Few people are willing to pay the short-term price for long-term success, but those who do are richly rewarded. Once they reached their goals, they contined to set new and more challenging ones.

GOALS: *Cont'd...*

The benefits of goal-setting are obvious. Goals are a high priority in almost every single success story you read. Effective goal-setting is an extremely powerful tool that makes almost anything possible - within reason. The effectiveness of goal-setting has been proven over and over again by successful people, and the best part is it's a skill that anyone can develop. If you're serious about success, determine what you want - your major, long-term goal. Write it down, define and refine it. Then write a step-by-step plan for reaching it. Realistic, clearly-written goals are usually what separate the successful from the also-ran. When you make a commitment to a goal, you'll find that instead of wishing you could be successful, you're moving closer and closer to achieving what you desire.

2. Take Action

SUCCESSFUL people are not afraid to take action. They are doers. One thing that separates the successful from the not-so-successful is that they knew what they wanted , defined their goals and were able to go after them. By taking action they were able to produce results. There are always people who are better educated, have more experience, more money, more talent, but it's the individual who takes action and makes things happen who becomes successful. Success usually eludes those who procrastinate or are afraid to make a decision. The ability to overcome procrastination and indecision is within everyone's reach. Successful people find the strength to make important decisions and then take action.

3. Enjoy Their Work

SUCCESSFUL people realize that a good portion of their adult lives is spent working, so they choose a career or business that brings them happiness, fullfillment and purpose. Because they take pleasure in what they do, they work hard and excel. For many, money is secondary to enjoying their work. Some started out earning next to nothing and have gone on to earn higher wages, while others realize they may never become wealthy at what they do, but they enjoy it too much to really care. There are plenty of people in this world who are financially secure but are unhappy and unfulfilled by their work. That is not success. The secret to success is being able to enjoy the way you earn your living.

4. Work Hard

THERE is no shortcut to success. It takes a great deal of hard work. Successful San Diegans worked longer hours, practiced more, were better prepared, made the extra effort, pushed harder and did a better job than the person next to them. Most say their hard work is a major reason for their success. Their goals were important to them; they were willing to pay the price required and work hard for what they wanted. When they were faced with obstacles, failures and adversity, they just rolled up their sleeves and worked harder until they persevered. It should be noted that nearly every successful San Diegan quoted in this book enjoyed their work and found it so rewarding that it seemed natural to work hard.

5. Burning Desire To Succeed

◆

DESIRE, coupled with meaningful goals, action and hard work usually results in success. Successful people who have an overwhelming desire for something have more energy, passion, commitment and purpose. They are able to accomplish the seemingly impossible. Their desire strengthens their focus on success and they are able to overcome incredible odds and adversity, allowing them to excel. They are energized, and that energy spreads to those around them. Desire is the energy that fuels them towards greatness and allows these inspired people to wake up earlier, work longer hours, practice harder and surpass others who lack the same passion. For someone with a strong enough desire, there is always hope.

6. The Ability To Persevere

MANY of the people in this book overcame limitations, setbacks and tremendous odds to become successful. They were usually not expected to be the best in their field. A few were told they didn't stand a chance of making it. Some had success and lost it, but were able to get it back. The thing they all have in common is perseverance and persistence. If the road was blocked, they looked for alternative routes, always working toward their goal. And they never stopped trying. They are strong, resilient people who took challenges head-on and won. They didn't listen if someone told them something couldn't be done or that they lacked the means to do it. Their motto was always "Never say die."

7. Self-Discipline

Usually the more self-discipline a person has, the more successful and contented they are. It takes self-discipline to maintain your focus on a goal. There are always negative and tempting forces trying to pull people away from realizing their long-term goals in favor of short-term gratification. It's the people who can stay focused and on course who are able to avoid this trap and strive for long-term satisfaction and success in career, relationships and business. Self-disciplined people are able to channel their time, energy, resources and money to the accomplishment of their goals. Self-discipline is not something you're born with, but those who learn it and practice it have a great advantage over those who don't.

8. Courage

EVEN successful people feel anxiety, stress and fear, but what makes them successful is their ability to use that fear to propel them on to greatness instead of letting it hold them back. They realize that by conquering their fears they are able to take the action necessary to succeed. People who let fear paralyze them cripple their chances for success. Everyone possesses the power to overcome their fears. Successful people did it by pitting themselves against their greatest fears over and over again until they eventually overcame them. Many also use preparation as a way to overcome anxiety. Once they were able to control their fears, they took the necessary and calculated risks that helped lead to success.

9. Ability To Manage Time

EVERYONE begins with the same number of hours in a day. How you use that time is what's important. If you take one day and compare how a successful person uses the time as compared to an ordinary person, the difference is substantial. When you multiply that by weeks, months and years, the difference between success and mediocrity becomes obvious. Because they set their priorities based on goals, the most productive thing for them to do at any given time is clear. They know how to plan, organize, delegate, take action and , when needed, they know how to say NO! By developing time management skills, successful people are able to have more time for their friends, family, fitness - and for themselves.

10. Positive Thinkers

THERE are really only three ways to look at life. You can be pessimistic, indifferent or you can maintain an optimistic outlook. Successful people almost always choose to be positive, hopeful and enthusiastic. They realize that life is a series of highs and lows, but they choose to focus on the highs. Optimism is a way of life - positive thinking brings positive results, and positive results make you more optimistic. Success rarely comes to negative thinkers, because they're too busy suffering from fear, anxiety and conflict. Because positive thinkers are generally happy people who emphasize the good in almost any situation, others are drawn to them and opportunities open to them that often elude others.

11. Live A Balanced Life

MANY successful people credit a balanced life as the reason for their success. Although they are extremely busy, most take the time to exercise and keep in shape, realizing that without their health, nothing else really matters. Many also credit their spouses for much of their success. These successful people realize that their families and friends are the sources of the most worthwhile and lasting satisfaction in their lives. They are driven when it comes to their work, but they also realize how empty success can be without someone to share it with. Sometimes the most productive use of your time is to take a vacation, sleep late, read a good book, enjoy your hobby, spend time with your family or simply watch the sun go down.

12. Ability To Overcome Adversity

ADVERSITY, frustration, discouragement, rejection and hardship are things that almost everyone will face at one time or another in their lives. How you handle it determines whether or not you will be successful. Winners are able to persevere and rebound from life's toughest challenges. They respond with courage, determination and faith to overcome enormous obstacles on their way to success. They are able to learn from failure and use adversity as an incentive to rise above and become stronger. This gave them the inspiration - the need - to strive for a better life and success. Successful people are resourceful and resilient and never quit in the face of tough challenges.

SUCCESSFUL SAN DIEGANS
The Stories Behind San Diego's Most Successful People, Both Past & Present

by Lee T. Silber
Foreword by Larry Himmel

This book contains the most complete collection of biographies ever written about San Diego's most accomplished and successful people in the fields of entertainment, sports, media and business. Included are over 100 full-length and in-depth profiles, as well as an additional 175 shorter biographical sketches. Many of those profiled are quoted in *Notes, Quotes & Advice*.

$15.95 • paper • 356 pages
ISBN 0-9628771-1-5

TO ORDER SEE ORDER FORM...

THE "SUCCESS IN SAN DIEGO" QUARTERLY NEWSLETTER

A quarterly newsletter for and about successful San Diegans

The competitive edge you need to succeed!

HERES WHAT YOU GET:

• Inspirational profiles of San Diego's most successful and famous people.

• Practical "what to do" and "how to do it" advice from respected leaders in their field.

• Motivational notes, quotes & advice.

• Updates on successful San Diegans and their latest accomplishments.

"The information in your newsletter is very interesting, thanks for keeping me up-to-date."
-- **Robert Price, CEO, Price Club**

FOR A COMPLIMENTARY COPY, SEE ORDER FORM ON NEXT PAGE...

ORDER FORM

TITLE	QTY.	PRICE	TOTAL
Successful San Diegans		15.95	
Notes, Quotes & Advice		6.95	
Combination of both books		19.95	

Shipping and Sales Tax Included **FINAL TOTAL**

Name:_____

Address:_____

City:_____

State/Zip:_____

❑ **Please send me a complimentary copy of the SUCCESS IN SAN DIEGO NEWSLETTER**
❑ **Please send me a SUCCESSHOP™ CATALOG**

TO ORDER BY MAIL
Send a check or money order with this form to:

TALES FROM THE TROPICS PUBLISHING CO.
P.O. Box 4100-186
Del Mar, CA 92014
619/792-5312

Please make checks payable to
Tales From The Tropics Publishing Co.

SPECIAL THANKS to **Ira Opper**, for your guidance and the example you set; **Larry Himmel**, whose encouragement is very much appreciated; **Michael McGeath**, I will never be able to repay you for your help; **Peter Karlen**, I hate to think where I would be without your sound advice; **Joseph Oppenheimer**, who is a wealth of wisdom; **Brian Tracy**, you have helped to spur me on to new heights I never thought were possible; **Anthony Robbins**, thanks for taking an interest in my success and offering your support; to **Rolf Benirschke** who is a truly nice person and a real inspiration; to **Robert Wade**, thank you for your kind words of support; **Mary-Ellen Drummond**, who always is there offering her help; to **Jimmy Buffett**, the role model I was finally able to meet; thanks **Mom** and **Dad** and a very special thank you to **Andrea**.

I would also like to thank **Roger Showley** of the Union-Tribune; **Woody Lockwood** at the Daily Transcript; **Angie Krause** at Channel 39; **Barbara Richards** at News Eight; and **Mary Hellman** at the Union-Tribune.

- Lee T. Silber
September 1993